B
in the
Night

Poems by
Richard Betz

For Martha

outskirts
press

Outskirts Press, Inc.
http://www.outskirtspress.com

ISBN: 978-1-9772-4307-2

Outskirts Press and the "OP" logo are trademarks belonging to Outskirts Press, Inc.

PRINTED IN THE UNITED STATES OF AMERICA

Table of Contents

FOREWORD
To a new voice in the world of poetry

"Life sings through our veins and unbalances us," remarks Richard Betz in acknowledging our mortality. "Perched on solid ground, clutching crook-neck canes, off-kilter, stumbling over our own feet, struggling with the undertow of simply being alive" is how he views the frailty of life.

Yet it's this very frailty that attracts Richard to each precious moment to be savored before it's gone, "pinching up every crumb of day" with "the taste of the purely physical on the tip of my tongue." It's what the Japanese call *Ichi-go ichi-e* (treasuring the unrepeatable nature of a moment).

His poems span the seasons from January to December and travel from the New England of his childhood to the Blue Ridge Mountains and Outer Banks of North Carolina.

In his companion poems "Stonework" and "Building Walls" he laments with nostalgia the loss that comes with the passage of time. "Work that endures" yields to "hard work and little to show for it." The same holds for words, which "skitter and slip like living things, like the dappled sunlight under these trees that shift and change when the wind blows." What he used to think he was good at, he still strives to achieve: "to enclose some small holy space," which he hopes to preserve in a poem.

He writes of a rainy day at the beach with *Il dolce far niente* (the sweetness of nothing to do), of fishing as a glorious waste of time, hands filled to overflowing with blackberries, the day-darkness of blindness, sand dollars broken into change, and the high bright cerulean sky.

His poems ring with the clink of cowbells, the clang of a hemlock branch on a metal roof, tick-tock crickets, the soft fall of a poplar petal into a cobweb, the rasping and screeching of iron on iron, the whispering water of fallen mountains, and the siren song of gravity. He paints what he sees and what he doesn't, the visible and the invisible, beyond the margin of sight.

His easel is filled with images of twig-legged shore birds, braids of foam, wind ripples of sand, pelicans stitching up waves, and the rumpled sea of a black snake on a windowsill, the ghostly blue lights of condo windows jumping with televisions, and the vast emptiness of a January sky.

His poems struggle with contradictions, as he confesses, "I learned to live with paradox." In seeking passageways from one world to the next, from doubt to faith, he writes of birth and death, the squaring off of religion and philosophy, the shedding of our belongings, blindness as a dilemma for the theologian, and the bewildered Lazarus stumbling unbound amongst us.

He finds inspiration for his poems in the *Bible* and Karl Barth, in the haiku, the poems of the Chinese Taoist Han-Shan, the plays of Shakespeare, Homer's *Odyssey*, the poetry of the Polish-American Miłosz, the songwriter Leonard Cohen, the artwork of the Japanese designer Ohara Koson, even the Japanese chef Masa Takayama, and Yogi Berra.

Richard writes with a delicate gentleness when he describes his daughter at birth, having "kissed the softest forehead my lips have known, and watched two eyes drift quizzically across mine." He writes with a merciless honesty when he describes the unkind, broken world of "The Wrong Things" and the raw, bitter, icy winter warmed only by candlelight at Christmas. Then there's the humor of "Bells in the Night."

He uses metaphor as a subtle tool of understanding, making it hard to tell "where metaphor ends and rock begins." Yet all his poems strive for the glorious insomnia of complete wakefulness, a waking up to the glories of nature but also to the glory of an oncologist's report that reduces a merciful day "to such absolute joy."

Randolph P. Shaffner
Retired Professor of English and Comparative Literature
Black Mountain, NC
November 8, 2020

Perfect Pitch

There may be nothing perfect after all
But my father's pitch pipe, The Master Key,
Nestled in its blood-red velvet-lined box,
That I inherited with his yellowed sheet music:

Its single brilliant clarion note – A440 –
That called so many *a cappella* choirs to order,
Snapping a dozen dozing ears to attention,
Pitched in the cavernous chancel silences.

It was the single slimmest arc of rising
Sun on the breathless ocean at dawn,
The first bright stitch, the audacious knot,
Prelude to the prelude in a puzzle of music.

He knew how rare true absolute pitch could be,
"One in a thousand," he would tell me,
To hit that note pure and unreferenced,
Archer's arrow shot true from tautness,

Poem un-baffled, without forethought or revision.
To see the world like that! – the sighing wind
Lifting the hemlock boughs with a gentle baton
As the great good choir begins to sing.

Splitting Oak

Would that every problem could so easily be parsed
As this stubborn piece of chestnut oak, *Quercus prinus*,
Hugging its heavy grain so close and tight
Around itself, resisting the many maul blows.

Here on this last day of winter, the very end,
I stand beneath a sky so filled with contradictions
That I can scarcely work: the bright sun burning
Through a flurry of late March snow,

Swirling around me in a dazzle of light,
Bright dancing bluster all around as I
Swing an eight-pound maul in cogent little arcs
Striving to comprehend this obdurate chunk of oak.

The sharp maul-edge bounces away, again and again,
From wood invulnerable to tempered steel.
Until, suddenly, there is a deep hollow tone,
Surprising and singular: a cry, a shout,

As if this piece of tree remembered summer thunder.
And in an instant there are two halves fallen,
Left and right, this and that. So. We do what we can,
Here on the edge of a sprawling wilderness;

The little axe falls and makes its little sound
In firewood's rough husbandry, a destructive force
Scattering pieces of a puzzle around me and
Disappearing in a bright blue column in the sky.

Shore Path, Bar Harbor Maine

It is no surprise that Balance Rock rests so effortlessly
On the edge of Frenchman Bay; despite the stiff wind,
It teeters not an inch, as if all clumsiness has been
Washed away from beneath it. The rocks around

Are deeply seamed, and it leans upon a small mesa,
Propped on a casual elbow to while away the eons,
Tilted improbably askew. Here it rolled down the side
Of Cadillac Mountain, and stopped, and moved no more,

Le mot juste, deftly penned, now resting in silence,
Just so. The geologists call it a precarious boulder,
Cousin to those tiptoe spire-top red sombreros
Weathering sandstorms in the Garden of the Gods.

But they are not precarious at all: they are dense
And immovable, like a lesson learned the hard way,
They will stand longer than a man will live.
It is we who wobble and sway and fall over:

Life sings through our veins and unbalances us,
Perched on solid ground clutching crook-neck canes,
Off-kilter, stumbling over our own feet, struggling
With the undertow of simply being alive.

It feels that way this morning on the Shore Path,
Where I practice my Tai Chi in the unsteady light,
Standing on one leg, just this side of faltering, mindful
Of my clumsy mortality, of my expertise in falling.

The White Peacock

The white peacock is thought to be an albino,
But it is nothing of the sort, ornithologists say;
It is a genetic variant of the Indian Blue Peafowl,
Pavo cristatus. Albinos are something else.

But that does not explain why it roosted here,
In this particular tree, high in the moon-bright sky
Screaming outside our window the long night
Like a fellow woman giving difficult birth.

It was Easter morning, and I marveled at this sight;
Three pine trees and this white bird in the middle,
Its long tail feathers dangling down in glory
Like a bridal veil. So I stood and beheld it,

I held it in my eyes, its import and portent
Eluding me a little in the calm morning light,
Where empty porch swings rocked in a gentle breeze
And lesser birds sang their incidental songs.

What brought this prodigy to roost here, on Easter,
Screaming at a man who has been studying Barth
And his impertinent question, *Is it True?*
Was it birth and death screaming in this tree?

Or was it just a figment of the ear, a bright surmise
Of bone and feather, a harmless coincidence.
A world with no pigment after all. Something else,
Roosting in the branches of this redoubtable tree.

4

Stonework

To lift these stones into sunlight,
To yank them from their fastness
Still wearing the musk of soil and darkness
These long eons, alone and lost,
The fragments of great mountains;

To mix mortar by hand, and to choose,
And fit them in the time-honored way,
Good footings and plenty of weepholes,
Two stones on one, one stone on two,
Fractures smooth along a true taut string:

This is work that endures,
More than name, occupations, frame dwellings,
Inheritance, wedding rings and silver,
Fistfuls of genes passed on to children,
Or any of the other ephemera of the seasons.

Stand firm, good wall,
In this sunlight into which I have called you
And the shadows of poplars not yet sprouted;
Dig in your heels and lean into the earth,
Thick with moss and thrift.

The Painter

I thought he was surf fishing,
Ghostly on the beach in sea mist,
But instead of a rod holder augured securely,
A delicate wooden easel balanced
On an elegant tripod, messy with paint.

His tiny oceanscapes are always
The same – the swirling turbulence,
The gleaming horizon, the braids of foam
Crouched in the narrow spectrum
Between azure and tarnished copper;

Capsules of wonder and grace:
He seems to greet with a glad hand
The contentious surf, day after day,
Miniaturist witness to the hollow tide,
A crooked smile crinkling his eyes,

Believing nothing but what he sees.
Postcard-small, inklings of paintings,
He pins them on the corner of the easel,
These tiny haikus, in lucid defiance
Of the immensity of ocean and sky.

Miller Cemetery

[For James Taylor Ramey]

All morning the clouds rushed overhead,
Driven by the west wind, but silent,
Like a howl that no one could hear:

Wind of grief, wind of sorrow,
Wind of no tomorrow.

In Miller Cemetery we gathered to pray,
Scripture under the swaying pines,
Consolation of wind and wind.

Downcast eyes note the long, unkempt grass,
Still green in January, terribly out of place,
And the dead leaves scattered loosely on top.

Never to have breathed this cool air,
Mineral damp beneath the high trees,
Nor felt this chill in the bone; never
To feel the bruise or the nail,
The tremble of fear, the tight knot
Of jealousy or rage, the pang
Of lost love, the cold slap of betrayal,
Or the vast emptiness of a January sky.

Wind in the trees, the tall pines
Swaying with a whisper barely audible;

Wind of grief, wind of sorrow,
Wind of no tomorrow.

Toad on the Walkway

I went out to look at the sky and the ocean,
Hazy Full Wolf Moon high overhead,
The humid saltwater air warmer than it should be
In January, when we expect hard sickle-edges.

Something fluttered overhead in the darkness
And I stumbled a little on the wooden walkway,
Illuminated by ghostly alternating lamps,
First on one side, then dimly on the other.

And suddenly there on the walkway beneath a lamp,
Out of the corner of my eye, a tiny creature
Hopping like a cricket: a toad, so small
He would have sat on the head of a penny.

Each crack between the boards was an abyss,
As he, too, stumbled along, speckled sand-colored
Hourglass outline on his back, measuring
His brief, crooked, fumbling path in the dark.

I knelt to see him more closely, and I thought
Beyond the dank dune grass and red cedars
I could smell the faraway fires of Australia,
Carried across a distant ocean and continent,

And I could hear off to the west the repeating boom
Of that big howitzer firing all day at Camp Lejeune,
And see the ghostly blue lights of condo windows
Jumping with televisions; and I knelt lower and lower,

Kneeling before this tiny, inconsequential amphibian,
Anaxyrus americanus, supplicant in the temple
Of the ordinary, a novitiate learning new prayers.
What do I know after all? Precious little.

Maundy Thursday

When all is said and done, it is a long way
From Jerusalem on this singular day in April,
The Bonaparte's gulls floating over the ocean
On a southerly breeze that bears no sign

Of suffering. Doctor of Divinity, tell me,
Why did the priest Jean-Marc Fournier
Rush into the burning Notre-Dame Cathedral
To save the Crown of Thorns? It could have

Perished under the collapsing timbers,
Relieving us of the remembrance of agony,
This reliquary of pain, this *mandatum* of blood.
High overhead a hawk-shaped kite is suspended,

In the same sky as the gulls and the clouds,
Bobbing up and down gently, its hawk-arms
Out-flung, tethered on an invisible string,
Like the call of church-bells, to believers

Or nonbelievers alike; or the memory of
Someone or something you used to love
That wakes you in the middle of the night.
Tell me, Doctor, have you walked out today,

Out the short walkway to the top of the dunes,
Where the sea oats are quivering in the breeze,
And children are running heedless with joy into
The abundant surf, the gracious wide-open ocean?

Bells in the Night

For want of the exact word
The moon stalled in a nether orbit,
Cast no light, was
As good as not.

The cowbells in my neighbor's pasture –
What did they do? Clink
Clink, to and fro: but
Nothing rang in my soul,

No tongue pealed in sympathy, nor
Sought my understanding. Instead these brutes
Walked through the very center of the world,
Climbing up and down the hill all night,

Waiting for the moon to come grazing
In silver clover.

Going Out to Watch the Stars

Going out to watch the stars,
I left my pencil behind:

My blank journal on an orderly desk
Lay still. The dog opened one eye

And listened to my footsteps,
The screen door bang and whirr of crickets.

She thinks, what can he be doing,
At this hour of woodsmoke and dew, alone?

The great poems of loss and rebirth
Remain unwritten. The voice is silent.

He stands on the front porch and watches
Familiar constellations revolve.

The Empire of the Eye

1.

Haloes around the streetlights and the moon
May have been the first inklings in that humid
Night. Though the body is tranquil and cool,
The eye can be cooking, ready to erupt.

My mother's letters charted his decline,
From that midday clarity reading faded Bach
Without flaw, to missed cues at the organ bench;
The humiliation of a license examination,

The traffic accidents cagily recounted,
Safe routes plotted down quiet streets.
And glasses as big as globes. The weather
Is cooler this week, the sky is clearer.

When he listens to music, he keeps his eyes
Closed tight, protective and private, as if
Nurturing sight behind eyelids without lashes,
Pink and delicate as a newborn's skin.

2.

How deeply we depend on all that we see.
From horizon to horizon, the Empire of the Eye:
The dazzle of daylight, the glance of inference,
Color and motion and endless variation.

And how penetratingly we dread darkness final:
To be permitted only to feel, not to see,
The brightness of the sun on one's face,
The texture of sea and sand curling around

Glimpses of shells: it would never be enough,
To be deprived of light explicit and direct,
Its throb and glory so profuse that it implants
Too much pressure for the eye to contain.

This boon, this excellence, this sight –
It is a paradigm of the quintessential light
That strikes us only glancingly, infrequently,
In a day that is forever half night.

Branch Drop

In the middle of a still night our hemlock tree
Woke us with a clang on the shed's metal roof,
So loud we thought it might have been more than
A single lower branch: Cladoptosis,

The shedding of branches no longer needed;
They prune themselves, they limb themselves up
In the dark of the night when it is easiest to let go,
Before the morning birds can raise any objection.

It reminded me of Barbara, who wanted less and less,
Who gave away everything these past few years,
Quietly and without a fuss, starting at the attic
And moving downward floor by floor, leaving

A gentle trail of broom-swept emptiness behind;
First her knitting, then her china; boxes and boxes
Of photographs of Italy, friends who were gone,
And finally – most difficult of all – her books.

But giving up comes easier with use, like any skill;
The rooms seemed to empty themselves, one by one;
Sunlight streamed into the curtainless house
And the floorboards gleamed brightly with loss.

The Way to Heaven is Broad and Catholic

Contrary to what the narrow men declare,
The way to heaven is broad and catholic.

It accepts the blue mountain snows,
Weird and rare from the winter stars;

The muddy creek choked with reeds,
Seep of ditches sour with cattle;

It murmurs in the shallow places
Where the sweet apple blossoms float;

It whispers generously among the reeds,
And seeks the lowest way.

Speak to me not of urgency or contention;
On the sunlit riverbank let us drowse.

Ode to Azomite

The Azomite from Amazon
Came promptly through the post;
All the way from Salt Lake City,
Nearly coast to coast.

I spread it on my garden beds –
Oh tell me what it means?
This ancient acronymic dust
Now scattered amongst my beans.

Thirty million years ago
Volcanic ash dispersed
Across an ancient inland sea
And settled in this verse.

It settled in my crooked rows
Across the breadth of time;
From fire to dust, now ending up
Remembered in these rhymes.

The Undiscovered Poems of Han-Shan

"Lu-ch'iu Yin then enlisted the aid of the monks in gathering together a number of poems which Han-shan had inscribed on trees and rocks or the walls of the houses and offices in the nearby village."

1.

The hawk from its perch on Cold Mountain,
Swept down into the valley, across the field,
And seemed to disappear into thin air,
As if by the power of its own grace
Escaping between two membranes in the afternoon
Into another place.

2.

To set events in motion,
However discretely;
To plant seed
With modest expectation:
That is great power.

To place one stone on another,
To raise a wall on
Good foundations;
To try to live deliberately:
That is true affirmation.

When winter solstice came,
We soaked a dozen blue spruce seeds
And lay them in a cold, dark place.
We slipped a hundred daffodil bulbs
Into the smiles sliced by the spade.

3.

I wanted to plant new apple trees,
And I thought that I could destroy these old pine trees
Today, in January, when they were fast asleep.
But the thick sap still flowed deep within them,
Its tang was in the air, and in the mayhem
Of trunks and branches slain flat.

4.

Night sky:
Flashlights pointing out the distant stars
Stumble over the bare branches overhead.

5.

These are the words that cure my incoherence,
That slake my thirst.

6.

Poems written on rocks and trees,
Read by the autumn fog and the falling leaves:

Who can separate them from the fastness
In which they were scrawled?
Who can tell where metaphor ends
And rock begins?

Old Salem

Golden ginkgos branch wide and
Close to the ground like gossip, or disease,

Running here in God's Acre,
Meandering among the silent graves,

Back and forth across this orderly document,
Reading name after name,

Row after row, column after column,
An imperturbable geometry of choirs.

How bright these leaves must have been
One hundred years long gone,

And how bright they will appear
To the solemn children who will come afterward,

Extravagant with saffron-colored light,
Extraordinary brightness:

Such glory in a place of death:
It is almost too much to bear.

Poor Stephen

"Rest, rest, perturbed spirit."– Hamlet, I, v.

Poor Stephen,
Chained to your chair,
Poor fallen Daedalus.

They tell me that once you soared,
You felt the sunlight on your wings,
The tremor in your loins.

But now you gaze at the mere cosmos
And sing the glories of the black holes,
The blue touch paper blown to ash.

I think of you when I am falling asleep,
And the cloud of silence gathers round,
The tick-tock crickets winding down,

The moon behind the trees, no sound,
Nothing but a hound in the distance
Locked in a furious argument with the night.

Wachet Auf

Sleepers wake,
Wake O Wake;
Loud call the voices of the watchmen.

I also watched, from the shadows of these dark curtains:
Heralds twittering in the bowing dune grass,
Insistent light replacing the immaterial stars,
Sudden revelation appearing over the horizon.

And the familiar widening path of sunrise
Processing in rippled splendor down its own aisle;
The liturgy of sunrise over the ocean
Is a comfort to those of us on-shore,

Reminding us of the death of darkness,
The surprise of joy, the power of discipline,
The irrepressible giggling in the youth choir:
A call to worship without shame or artifice.

What is a good Presbyterian to do?
I filled out the little card in the pew,
Asking the Pastor to come and visit me again
And explain to me why we must suffer so on Sundays,

When the morning wrens sing so flawlessly
The glorious counterpoint, the exalted lyric,
And the basso continuo of the booming surf:
O Doctor of Divinity, I shall never want to sleep.

A Soft Target

I have come to understand that I am an old man,
A soft target, open to the accidental atrocity;
I sit at my table on an innocent cafe terrace
Under a harmless pastel umbrella.

All my locks have been disengaged,
All my passwords have been hacked.
It is so easy to turn me into a casualty
When my life is so open and I am unafraid;

I cannot be terrified anymore, not even by
The silence at three a.m., the hollow chimes at noon,
The darkness in hearts that I don't understand,
The unseen murderer waiting around the corner.

These are contingencies I cannot change,
My helpless complicity with life. But now, see:
Evening has brought a youthful blush to the sky;
The night-air is heavy with savory cooking,

A man with a guitar is playing a blue little song.
I savor my glass of Pinot Gris, surrounded by
A truce of friends, and children, and laughter.
In the distance I hear the tinkle of broken glass.

Violet

They made fun of your name, you said,
Faithful Violet, raised Down East,
The sandy soil as flat as the beach, yet
Far from the balm of cool ocean breeze.

Tobacco barns on the edge of the field,
Shacks huddling under scant trees;
I have driven through this unforgiving land
But never wanted to linger long.

I remember visiting your kinfolk here,
In the lowly places where they lived, out
In the open fields in shimmering heat;
We were from another country, and I was

Shocked by their floors of simple dirt.
Scarcity was a chair pulled up to the table,
An unwelcome guest who had to be fed.
They waste nothing who have nothing to waste.

Who was it taught you to braid rugs from
Scraps of cloth, make pickles from watermelon rind?
The few keepsakes you owned – the mysterious
English urns, the silver bowl that christened a PT Boat,

The framed poem, *The Old North State*,
That hung in the bedroom wherever you lived –
Were priceless treasures you rescued from nothing,
Keepsakes propped against a wall of dispossession.

Here's to the land of the long-leafed pine,
The summer land, where the sun doth shine;
Where the weak grow strong. From this scant
Dirt, in the dry pine needles, violets flourish.

Broken Beyond Repair

Jack of all trades, master of one or two,
I found it hard to accept that anything could be
Broken beyond repair. There's always duct tape,
And strong glue; soothing words before sleep,

And long walks on this wide beach,
Our footprints behind us a crooked seam
Where the waves are gently breaking.
Every sand dollar is broken into change,

Every whelk is a shattered crown,
The shell hash broken finer and finer
With every tide. The living shifting beach
Is a fresh wound, a temporary accommodation

Between the ocean and the mainland,
Abandonment and reunion. These sand dunes
Are fortified by donated Christmas trees,
A fragrant heritage buried deep beneath our feet.

This is what we do, we handymen:
We patch things up as best we can;
We try to keep it all from blowing away
In wind ripples of sand. We cannot accept

The ring of finality, the sorrow that cannot be
Redeemed, the glimmer of hope: a little glue,
A little attention, to hold back the tide, to silence
The unbearable song of the wind.

Sea Glass

They say you don't find sea glass,
Sea glass finds you. But I am a skeptic,
So I looked for it every day in the jumble
Left by the tide: the mermaids purses
Containing nothing by the end of day,
The hollow shells, the crab shells picked clean;
The insufficient ocean shying away.

Seeking has an undertow of its own,
Seductively sliding away beneath your feet
And carrying you out to sea like those
Forgotten bottles: the bright brown beer,
The aquamarine coke tumbled smooth,
Redeemed from their brokenness.
Finding can be a reward of its own.

Looking for something I had never yet found,
I expected that I would startle the singular object,
The bright precious sparkle of the extraordinary,
That my shadow would overpower it there
On that little strand between these two worlds,
And that I could put it in my pocket to keep.
I imagined that we might find each other at last.

Cervices

I cut a circle in a piece of paper.
Ten centimeters across – four fingers.

I tacked it high on the house beam
Where it hung all day like a new moon.

All day April bloomed into May.
The petals of the dogwood fell on the road,

I lay in the sun under a deep blue sky
While a high, lazy jet crossed overhead

In a straight line east to west, and I
Watched its vapor trail slowly disappear

Like an incision healing without a scar,
Thinking of that little circle, and marveling

How narrow the passageways are
From one world to the next.

A Daughter

Tonight I held fragile in the rough
Crook of my arm love's unequivocal
Proof, the seal of faithfulness. I kissed

The softest forehead my lips have known,
And watched two eyes drift quizzically
Across mine. I touched pink lanolin feet

And long fingers wrinkled and sage;
Eyelashes that, if sound, would be quieter
Than whispers, than lips merely moving,

Yes, I held in my hands an innocence so
Complete, a youth so perfect, I stroked
Eyebrows so ineffable, that this touch

Lingers on my hands for hours afterward,
And I realize that hereafter they can do
Nothing but gentleness.

Peace and Plenty

1. Duck, April.

At this little house at the end of the road
There seems to be plenty. Enough
Is plenty: plenty of sea-grass and sand

And the long horizon stretching out north and south,
The ever-moving ocean speaking and speaking,
Advancing and receding in white foam.

2. Easter Sunrise at the Kitty Hawk Pier.

Trumpets greet the resurrection sun –
Hundreds of worshippers gather and scatter
To hear a learned doctor preach the gospel,
Quoting from memory Tennyson and Browning,
And affirming once again truth and life.

Worshippers say the crowds grow
More and more each year:
The net can barely contain them.

3. Currituck Beach Lighthouse.

A thin white sail out on the horizon:
Perhaps this mariner will be cautioned
By the flashing beam, powered by
Weights and chains as it scans the sea,

The lightkeeper cranking up the weights
Every two-and-a-half hours. It is seldom safe

To come ashore along these miles of coast.
Praise God for safe harbor.

4. *Peace and Plenty.*

So this man too escaped the dirty fates
That claimed so many ships along this shore,
Full sail on the high seas, thus far eluding
The ordinary obligations, Scylla and Charybda

Of birth and death, from cape to cape,
The weed-choked latitudes, halcyon longitudes,
And the wide desolation of the open sea,
Navigating by the distant stars,

To this place of Peace and Plenty:
Now, here, the salt breeze, the flashing sun
Reflected in the surf, his wife by his side,
His daughter's footprints dimpling the sand.

Far Off Hatteras Point

The amnesia of open water.
How we can forget
that we once stood
on solid ground,
on the verity
of unmoving earth.

The horizon that never
burgeons into land.
The beak that returns with nothing.
Vagrant rocking
on the unavailing waves.
We can almost remember.

The hope of safe harbor,
sheltered water ringed round
with pastel cottages;
mending nets, tending gardens
day by day.
I have forgotten how to be afraid.

The rapture of forgetfulness,
how we are
So far away.
How we are
just a tiny light,
fallen on the horizon.

Nets Flung Wide

1. *Thunderstorms*

So we find ourselves at Peace and Plenty again
This early Spring, the surf too cold to swim.
Here on this barrier island, instead of in London,
Trying to find some peace in the midst of war,
And plenty amidst an understanding of want.
The surf rolls in without relenting, wave
After wave, pounding like artillery,
And the night sky lights up suddenly from time
To time, all of a piece, as if lit from behind,
With flashes of lightning. The wind moans,
Carrying sheets of water, waves of violence,
As we sit by the hearth fire and ponder
The enormity of weather, and its implacable power
Over the just and the unjust.

2. *Faith*

In the bookstore in Manteo
Philosophy and Religion stand back to back,
As if squaring off to fight a duel – ten paces, turn.

Closer inspection revealed deceit – this is not
True philosophy at all but postcards from the Orient,
Not religion but cross-stitch patterns, home sweet home.

Has the age-old dispute finally ended this way?
The rock of salvation and the ocean of possibility
Reduced to a stubborn standoff, false to false.

Here along the shoreline they work out their differences
In uneasy rhythms: breaking waves, skittering birds,
Sheets of foam, and ever-shifting sand.

3. *Laughter*

The shore seems like a graveyard today,
Littered with the delicate spines of fish, tiny skulls,
Long necklaces of whelk-egg casings,
The incinerated coin-purses of kites; crab shells,
Chunks of helmets and armor, and bones,
Everywhere, crushed bones. Segments of straw
Hop end to end in the shore-breeze,
And the coastal sea – Graveyard of the Atlantic –

Is ultramarine dark and cold. When suddenly
Two glistening porpoises leap from the depths
Into bold light and foam, thrashing like lust –
Like sudden laughter interrupting a grim sermon.

Pay attention, Preacher: even you
Can still be surprised. The beach grass in the wind
Has described perfect circles in the sand.

4. *Fishing*

In the bookstore in Corolla
Christianity stood back to back
With Fishing/Boating,

But in a comradely way, each watching
The other's back. The nets
Flung wide.

Fishing:
What a glorious
Waste of time.

The Sweetness of Doing Nothing

Rainy day at the beach and nothing to do,
Il dolce far niente. Rain streaks the porch screen,
Leaving little strands of dangling pearls.

The deck boards are wet and glistening dark,
And they make an indecent sound as I walk,
Slap-slap, step-step. My bare feet.

Nothing to do. But watch and listen;
So I go outside and stand in the rain,
Squinting up at the blinding gray dazzle

Where suddenly a long strand of pelicans flying
Appears overhead, as if released from stone,
Fragments falling away in shards of blindness,

Falling from south to deliberate north,
Huge and silent in the high tilting air:
Nine, twelve, gazing down at the water,

Following a meandering, narrow periphery
Between Pamlico Sound and wide open water,
Reading the eddies and the shadows below.

Their eyes are as big as the ocean,
As big as the horizon, sliding down crookedly
In the rapture of the sweet morning rain.

Just Above the Surface

1.

On the way to the Outer Banks
Our new tires on the freshly-scored asphalt
Just outside of Charlotte, moaned like the
Songs of whales.

2.

We arrived, as in the past, on the heels
Of a cold front. A stiff gale blew all night:
Deck chairs rattling against the rails,
Canvas and sea grass and palm fronds bent
Horizontal in the leveling wind, and
Beneath everything the great moaning and
Whistling undercurrent, the symphony of wind.

Waves breaking north to south, diagonally,
Instead of east to west.

Eight brown pelicans winged single file
Just above the surface.

3.

What harm can there be in enjoying these days?
The cool breeze wafting over us as we lie
In horizontal chairs, the sound of the surf
So final and endless.

We walk and regard
These shells, spines and skeletons washed up

On the shore. Day so brilliant that we awaken
Long before sunrise, not to miss
A single golden moment of this voyage
Between two shores.
Not to think:
Just to let the hours wash over us.

4.

The moon rose finally, lower later
Than I had predicted, as if delayed
By an unavoidable accident. Dim and shaken,
It struggled over the horizon, stumbling slowly
And wearing a ludicrous pumpkin-colored robe
Borrowed at the last minute from something the
Setting sun had cast off.
Finally, as night wore on,
It came into its own, shedding the traces
Of day, shining with the same celestial light
As the distant stars.

5.

At last the wind has died down, the passion
Of the ocean has waned: fine-textured
It shrugs each wave easily ashore.
Mewing gulls wheel and dance, no longer
Stricken like kites against the gale,
And the twig-legged shore birds scamper
Easily between the waves.

Not to think,
Merely to glory in the common miracle,
The guileless surface of things: no sign
Of an ominous undertow.

36

On the far side of the world a war is being fought,
Children strapping bombs to skinny chests,
And Christ crucified in a theatre near you.
Still, the pink light of morning insists,
It demands our attention, painting each house
With peace and plenty.

6.

At high tide, just after sunset, some
Painterly clouds brushed lightly pink,
And the sea as still as I have seen it,
Barely lapping at our toes. Pale blue sea,
Black eyebrow waves, a garland of foam:
It seemed to be the final reach of some
Large exertion, failing again, and called
Back into itself. A bulging of surface,
Bursting with things to say, falling into
Whispers and silence.

7.

The sun this morning rose bright and uncomplicated,
Wide golden path straight to shore.
Small groups of birds winged north to south,
South to north, crossing the golden meridian.

8.

Eyes closed in the sun, listening, my breath
Almost synchronizes with the breaking waves;
Eating and sleeping, low tide and high:
The daily rhythms of life at its most elemental

Find common origin in the tide-tugged ocean.
Perhaps that is why its call is so insistent.
Lofty thoughts seem far away. Here
There is only the endless commotion,
Wave after wave after wave.

The Birder

This birder knew his grackles from his grebes;
He rarely needed to lift his binoculars to his eyes,
His huge sad eyes, full moons behind oversized rims
That took in the landscape so comprehensively.

Here on Yarrow's Loop there was a little swamp,
A few bare trees; it was a good place to spot an ibis,
And the yellow-rumped warblers were so plentiful
They kept away the plovers and the painted buntings.

That was what I admired the most: how this birder
Knew their names, the fine distinctions; not just warbler
But black-throated green, hooded, black-and-white,
Mature and immature, greater and lesser warbler.

Surely that is the only instruction we require:
To give names to the parts of a world, to this place,
And the little harbors and sounds all along the coast.
Earlier this morning the sky and the ocean were one,

Joined together in a single undifferentiated horizon;
But now there was a sharp line drawn, white and clean,
Between this and that. Do we have a name for
The joy that we feel when the shroud of fog rolls away,

Or when the night heron rises in exultant flight?
The sadness that we feel when the distant freighter's
Sounding horn makes that desolate sound, as if
There is only this single bright flash of feather.

The Poem I Wish I Could Write

The poem I wish I could write
Would begin imperceptibly: slowly,
One would become aware of motion
High in the branches of an ancient oak –

A tree so vivid and specific
On this chiaroscuro day in early April
That you would see each crinkly caterpillar leaf
On the verge of opening—

Yes, there would be motion, high
In the crown of this vernal tree:
The wings of a large, fantastic bird
Shuddering like wet umbrellas shaken dry,

And opening at just the right moment,
A dark shape disappearing in unerring flight
Into the distances of the day, leaving behind
A single branch swinging to a stop.

Where to Begin Again

"Nothing is like it seems,
but everything is exactly like it is." – Yogi Berra

1.

Eight pelicans, single file, glided along a wave,
As deliberately as sentences appearing on a page:
I wondered where to begin again, here again,
On the outer edge of the only world,
Where sky and ocean are so large, where
Waving grasses, shifting sands, shells along the shoreline,
Make such convenient metaphor in what they seem,
So close and familiar. Yet so implacably remote.

2.

I wondered where to begin again, and so I began
With the idea of order. Eight pelicans, evenly spaced,
Could be reduced to the dynamic of flight,
The intricacies of flock and convocation,
Intimate knowledge of tides and spawning grounds.

But they flew so close to the lip of the wave
That they seemed to stitch up the ocean, to bind
Offshore and onshore, the shallow and the fathomless,
Making the disparate elements whole again:
Quick light flecked along the edges of their wings.

3.

I brought the idea of physics and biology
To the line demarcating the horizon,
The dune grass bending in the slender breeze;
The centrifugal whorl of the mollusk,
The tiny fan of the scallop shell on my finger-tip;
Refraction of the rising sun on the dappled ocean,
Pointing to the apex of many triangles,
And the cool, distant clouds layered in gold.

4.

I gazed at the geometry of incoming waves,
Surface on surface, translucent planes edged with froth,
Sliding one over the other like sloppy arguments,
Spilling in awkward shapes across the sand,
Yet contributing in some way to a grand explanation
That seemed larger than the parts of a world,
A theological thesis made of the sparest elements
Of water and sand. A small brown song sparrow
Landed on a thick stem of beach grass,
And I watched it bend, and bend, until it stopped.

The little bird eyed me with its tiny eye,
Then sprang away from bending stem.

5.

At night, the stars burned dimly in the watery sky,
Competing with the Kitty Hawk Pier, the Corolla Light.
Lights were blazing, too, in the house next door,
Where eight middle-aged women were playing cards

And growing slightly drunk on white wine. I stood
Watching them in the dark, sprawled on disorderly chairs,
Laughing and sighing at stories I could not hear,
So close that I felt I was in the same room.

Petal Fall

Into a cobweb so fine that it quivered
In the slightest breath of morning breeze
Had appeared a petal fallen to this place
From our tulip poplar, *Liriodendron tulipifera*,

Fallen from those inaccessible heights
To rest cradled like a child in a hammock,
Suspended between two beams of our pergola
It could have missed the mark so widely,

This unrepeatable, poignant descent
Through thick air from dizzying heights
Into ordinary days, fluttering down randomly
Like the path of a wayward swallowtail,

This way and that way, so errantly that
We might mistake it for a kind of order
Instead of this mere temperate descent
Into early summer air ringing like bells,

This sweetness of petals. Anthony told us that
The tea leaves had a sweet, innocent fragrance, too,
That day in Japan, when his friend Masa told him about
Ichi-go ichi-e – one time, one meeting.

I thought of him then as I studied this one petal,
Soft as peach-skin, dimpled lime green around
A tiny fan of apricot, falling into a cobweb,
This one time; only once. And never again.

44

Little Craft

I am always the last to bed
And the first to rise.

Nightfall with its owls and moons,
The hemlocks sighing, and the wind that cannot be
      consoled;

Daybreak with light seeping in the windows,
Coffee brewing in the kitchen;

And between these poles I linger and I listen,
This magic hour before the old dreams arise,

And the adventure begins again, strange and new –
Here in the shoulder time each day brings,

I drink sacramental coffee, I practice my Tai Chi,
I conclude and initiate, like the ferryman

Going from one shore to another,
Back and forth.

Great is the river and deep and wide
Bearing us up in our frail little craft.

Last Week in April at the Outer Banks

1.

Last week in April at the Outer Banks,
Gazing once again at the expanse of ocean,
Each wave unhurriedly displacing the next:

Two gulls fly low, just above their shadows,
On the swell of foam that each wave makes
As it nudges the next one gently ashore;

And from time to time the languid wash of hours
Slows so much that the ocean seems to stop, and
Skip a beat; the break of surf falls silent in one long

Coincidental moment: even the little shore birds
Pause in their twitterings along the top of the dune,
And the gulls observe a moment of silence

Before returning to their argument with the sea.
Finally the next wave draws a deep breath, and the rhythm
Of one thing following another is restored.

2.

A pair of dolphins comes close to shore;
Now each wave seems to hold a playful secret,
A dorsal fin appearing here, and there,

Upcurving in the glistening air, like the top
Of a dolphin wheel poking just above the surface
Turning round and round in this sunny realm.

The lip of each wave is as dark as iodine
And as bright as sunlight, dark and light and dark.
In come the waves, one after another,

Pushing and stumbling in the tumultuous surf.
The tide is going out, and the undertow is strong
The rough sand undermining all around

In the shaky equilibrium of the shore,
This momentary balance between earth and sea,
Light and dark, secret and revelation.

3.

A gale rises up in the night, the wind whines,
It moans unsettlingly all around this little house,
And shakes it back and forth on its narrow pilings,

Banging the loose gate on the deck,
Each gust harder than the last, until at its climax
It drowns out the booming of the surf.

Rain sizzles horizontally against the windows –
Or is it the sea, leaping from its appointed limit,
Trailing long streams of sea-foam in the darkness?

Lightning springs up all around, flashing bright
In all the windows at once, as if we are a little boat
Surrounded by mountainous waves of light.

Shaking on its pilings, anchored in mere sand:
We lie in each others arms all night,
Tottering somehow through these unexpected storms.

Running Over a Squirrel

Who could not admit the possibility
That by God's grace this squirrel survived
The hazards of a hundred wheels; that in
His providence he scurried from shoulder
To shoulder, bounding in the cool safe grass,
Up and up the vertical, chattering madly to the sky?

Until tonight, when I in my chariot of steel
Bore down helplessly upon him as he swerved and
Skittered, from side to side, finally ending up
Struck by my wheel, and in my rear-view mirror
Tumbling and tumbling and tumbling,
Tripping in astonishment over that graceful tail.

I cried to him without thinking, I'm sorry:
Sorry for the pain and the indignity, sorry
For bringing your harmless acorn-gathering,
Cat-chiding, chattering little life to such an
Inglorious end, your soft white belly turned up
In mute, vulnerable, uncharacteristic trust.

I too have gathered sweet acorns in the dusk,
And stood on high limbs gazing at the golden skies,
And watched the leaves burn with color each year.
And so I mourn for you, warm-blooded like me, and yet
Not like me, not daring to hope, nor empowered by
The blessings of love, the unparalleled gift of language,

The Near Journey

[For Mike McCall]

Why do you think it is a long journey,
Pastor Carl? You, a man of God, should know
How close and familiar it is, how deftly
We pass from one realm to another:

So near as to be opaque, a paper screen,
Behind which we can see the dim shadows
Of those who have already made that passage,
So easily, in the blink of an eye.

The History of Sight

In the beginning I was like the blind man in the Gospel;
People looked like trees walking. And then I saw
My Mom's face, and the cat who slept in my crib.
Thursday the sky was high bright cerulean;
Sunday vision fell like rain and puddled out.
I thought I saw like everyone else, even when
Shadow-shapes flitted in the corners of the yard
And God rays fell slantwise in the twilight.

I sat first row to read the blackboard before I knew
The boys in the back could see it just as well:
Nearsighted, everything a blur except the little toys
That I turned and turned to examine up close,
The marble puzzle, the clock I took apart and
Left in springs and gears for another time.
And then they gave me *corrective* lenses,
And like a strange drug it sharpened shapes:

In the exhilaration of heightened vision I thought
I could see forever, to the edge of the earth.
I did not know what day-darkness was until
My Dad lost his sight – glaucoma, too late –
And I learned there were edges you could fall off;
And how to let bright pearl-drop medicine dangle
And fall into my thirsty eye. I learned about
Trabeculectomies, and cataracts. Precious sight:

I close my eyes tight in the darkened room,
And shooting stars crawl forward, everything
Crawls forward, my Dad in blindness totters
Slowly up the aisle, holding my Mom's arm,
Groping for the organ bench in his little church,
Toeing the dark pedals, finding Middle C,

And playing the hymns he knew by heart
In blaze of sight that conquers blindness.

Another Funeral

[For Fred Reiter]

There are too many flowers. Yellow mums, salmon
Gladiolas, too many and too bright. They overwhelm
The man I knew, albeit slightly, and the
Occasion for which we have gathered.

But these are the objects attendant upon him now,
The images proposed for Presbyterian closure:
The casket, paisleyed gray on gray, draped with roses
Trailing four wide ribbons: MY. BELOVED.
HUSBAND. FRED.

The casket is cradled on a big brass dolly, scissored-
Out, on wheels like little tricycles. It is
Difficult not to notice these details: the cloying
Bouquets, the breeze stirring up wisps of hair,

The stubborn sanctuary clock, stopped at a quarter 'til,
Tottering on its thin blade of irony; and
Outside, through the open windows, the shrieks
Of daycare pre-schoolers, running and swinging, and

The high, keening, plaintive squealing of the
Merry-go-cycle – six tricycles welded together –
Groaning and grinding like some ancient sorghum mill,
Round and round. A few late arrivals slip in,

And everyone on the pew bobs up and down in little
Arpeggios, like muted hammers on the baby grand,
Maintaining carefully the required adjustments,
The delicately preserved spaces between each and each.

Suddenly, all rise – it always surprises me – and
Turn to face the family filing in from the rear.
A cheek is kissed, a hand is lightly covered,
And a child in arms begins, uncertainly, to sing.

One of the grandchildren plays a little prayer
On a silver flute, and it is this human melody,
Sweet and simple and unaccompanied, that finally
Opens my heart, and draws forth my sorrow.

Rest now, good and faithful servant, beyond our stanzas.

Two Haikus

1. Haiku on Poetry

Think what we may catch
In the holy limpid depths
With our net of words.

2. Haiku on Falling Leaves

Often letting go
Makes us rise instead of fall:
Lovely paradox.

Morning Glory: A Song of Innocence

It wants to climb,
This little vine,
Ascend to sky
And distant sun;

Deny the ground
From which it came,
Struggle free
Into light and air;

Bright green braid
Upward and away.
Amount to some
Thing after all.

The Umbrellas of the Morticians

[For Forrest Traylor]

The rain begins as quietly as disbelief,
Reluctant to make a sound above a whisper.

It is raining. It is a condition we accept.
Doors open briefly; windows stay closed.

The grave is down at the edge of the woods;
The hill is steep. I stand balanced a long time

On a little tuft of grass: here the whole afternoon
Seems a little out of plumb –

The averted trees, the angular rain,
Attentive chairs under a bright green canopy.

The sod has been cut and laid up neatly,
A little wall, off to the side.

Simple words are spoken. Under the umbrellas
We stand and listen singly, in twos or threes;

Several people share two umbrellas.
A dark-haired girl stands under the edge,

Her long hair twizzling down in tight curls
Like incense unraveling.

The umbrellas of the morticians float
Like big black ashes in the rain.

The Black Snake on the Windowsill

Unexpected as the midnight phone
I did not expect to see this deep crack up here,
So profoundly out of place.

There it lay on the windowsill,
Long and black like a silenced oboe.
I thought it must be a prank, a toy of doubt:

I refused to believe. But suddenly it was real:
Black ice on the road one morning.
The blind driveway. The effrontery of death.

Up, and up, it had reached this place,
Half its length still curled round the stone column below.
Not under the shady umbrellas of the summer squash,

But here, peeping and sleeping and creeping,
Implacably taking in our dinner table conversation
Softly lit in the gathering dusk.

The Upward Trail

When I began to climb the upward trail
The day was young, the morning sun was bright.
I took nothing with me. I expected little.
This is the place where I first stopped to rest,
And foolishly drank the last of my fresh water.
I remember the dragonflies, the Sistine sky overhead.
Every bend in the path was another riddle to ponder.
But I learned to live with paradox, One word at a time,
Step by step, I ascended the vocabulary of morning.

I left everything behind. I regretted nothing.
Morning birdsong made the difficult climb easy.
Soon I reached the first heartbreaking overlook,
And from the bare rock I could see forever:
The rolling ground falling away dizzyingly
To the hidden seas beyond the haze of morning,
And a single peregrine falcon suspended aloft
Surveying all below him with perfect clarity.
And I, too, wanted to achieve that summit of sight,

So I continued to climb, above the hardwoods,
High into the fragrance of the balsam afternoon.
Mile markers falling away behind me like the days.
At last, too late to return, I came to the upper place:
Bare rocks in the myrtle like a ruined temple.
Light falling behind the distant mountains,
Vesper hymns sighing through the trees.
Infinity of stars. Crooked smile of moon.
At last. The journey had begun.

The King of Metaphor

The King of Metaphor rides into the city
On a broad-backed mule. The mule's ears
Are soft and downy, and they turn and turn,
Attentive to every hush and murmur
In the humid air. His back is flat and plain,
And the cowlicked hair lies down in patches
In an intricate disorder, brushed every which-way
By the burdens he has carried.

Clop, clop:
Hooves on the flinty rocks, little pebbles
Rolling away. He does not wear a bell today,
Nor any adornment. The musky memory of manure,
The stiff tail swatting the persistent flies.
A calm hand at the withers, a quiet voice,
Asks, "Is it enough? Is it adequate?"

The mule's ears turn this way and that way,
The little pebbles roll away with every step.

Fragments for Another Day

1. *For my father's birthday: July 13, 1918.*

I know in my heart it is true,
That eyesight is a scarce commodity,
A household item that we consume like coffee.

My father peered from goggles that made his eyes look
Huge, as he read those tiny notes on the staff.
Smaller and smaller, less and less: degeneration.

But may there not be other kinds of sight? Sight in the
    dark,
Foresight and hindsight. Once he dreamed he saw the
    time
On a clock on the wall, and when he awoke it was exactly
    that time.

Now I sit, Sundays at the keyboard, just like him,
Binocular. Research for the ophthalmologist
And a dilemma for the theologian.

2. *A phrase I wish I could use in a poem.*

Like the visiting magi,
We returned to our own country by another route.

3. *At the Outer Banks.*

The tousled head of morning.
The rumpled sea.
The ambiguous sky refracting red.

The measured tides.
The feckless shore birds.

4. *Spring poem.*

I made a covenant with Spring.
It was Ordinary Time, and the crocuses were up;
The morning sun lapped at the edge of the pond.
And the birds sang every morning. I gave them
Literary names: Cheever Cheever Cheever.

Revival

Why do you conclude that the great event happened
At noon, when the desert sun casts no shadows?
No, Lazarus was raised on a cold and foggy night,
Dim torches in the distance sizzled in the dark,
Their haloes floated down the long hill to the tomb.

Did a loud voice cry out in the darkness?
If it did, we could not understand what it meant
Vague forms moved about in the shadows and the mist.
Once we thought that we felt through the ground
The rumble of the mighty rock being rolled away,

And then we smelled the rot, and the sweet nard,
Close and oppressive on the humid air;
And the women wailing and crying – with
Joy or with fear, we could not tell – and
The baffled shouting and commotion as they

Returned, leading the revived one in the darkness.
It was long ago, and now the grave is closed;
All we can remember with certainty (is it enough?)
Is darkness and fog, strange cries in the night, and
Bewildered Lazarus stumbling unbound amongst us.

Cleaning Out the Culvert at Hidden Springs Lane

Tell me again how deeply I need to dig.
The rhododendron grows so densely here
That the water barely reflects daylight: darkly
This branch meanders through the leaf-strewn woods,
Rolling smoothly over moss-covered stones.

Here at the culvert I wiggle the point of the spade
Slowly into the oncoming water, coaxing
Its patient power around the blade,
And lifting each load of dripping sediment:
It is like a poem being written one line at a time
With but a single purpose in mind.

Metaphor is not mere similitude –
Little pebbles glistening, jewels spilling recklessly
From the treasure chest of fallen mountains –
But a tool of apprehension:
I thrust the blade deeply into the whispering water
Not as high-minded example, or pleasure,

Not as deconstruction or edification,
But merely to clean out this culvert again,
The ordinary maintenance of the extraordinary,
Freeing this water to run clearly, as it gathers
Incremental strength on its way to distant seas.

Pruning the Apple Trees

I have pruned these trees before in gentler years,
When the sun was warm and my father was alive;

I have staked them straight, and angled crooked branches
Precisely with old wooden clothespins.

The principles of pruning are as immutable
As the will to thrive and the need to discipline:

Cut the bud at the branch tip and those behind it awaken;
Thwart the leader at its apex and branches spread wide.

Do not be afraid. Hold the pruning shears in a
Confident hand: Clip clip, clip clip:

The little branches fall away, the sun
Breaks bleakly through the morning haze.

Deer Crossing

The deer crossed the road – a young doe –
As suddenly as a stone skipped on bright water,
Breaking into my lazy morning reverie.

She did not hesitate, but leapt across unerringly,
As surely as anything I knew – as surely as
An accident, a coincidence, an unavoidable encounter,

Like rope snapped out taut, an event in time and place
One knew could not have been circumvented.
How unlike us: headlong with grace,

Plunging down the steep slope and out of sight;
Not choosing her footing carefully
As the theologians do.

Betula Lenta

Sweet Birch, *Betula lenta,*
Leaning over the babbling waters:
I fix you with the label exact,
Here in the depths of this little wood.

There is a bridge that spans the creek
And a path that winds between the trunks;
That is the way I have come this morning,
Expressly, with a map in my hand,

With two brass screws and a piece of plastic,
To bring some taxonomic order to this place.
Silently, your long trunk leans, and leans,
High over Mill Creek, climbing away.

Mercy

[For Dave Buck]

I found myself behind him one summer afternoon,
And fretted impatiently until I knew who it was,

Driving his big rusty car down Main Street,
Bald and inscrutable as a Buddha,

Taking the afternoon off,
Taking his time, elbow out the window.

So I slowed, too, and rolled my window down:
Summer drone of insects, soft balm of rustling leaves;

In the distance, a single songbird
Kept singing and singing, over and over.

I breathed deeply, suddenly hungry
For every fragrant breath of merciful day.

Why does it take an oncologist's report
To reduce the day to such absolute joy?

Under the shade trees, his car floated by,
Dappled with peaceful light. And I envied him.

Easels in the Garden

Easels in the garden, brushes in hand
On a Saturday in Edenton, *en plein air*:
The golden morning mimosa sunlight
Bubbled down through the dogwood trees.

Paintbrushes were clasped gently in deft hands,
Hands that yesterday wore petite flowered gloves,
Yanked weeds, deadheaded buds. Miss Francis
Succors the *Homestead's* roses with ruthless pruning:

Hundred-year-old roses in an antebellum garden –
And why should a rose live longer than a man? –
In this briefest of seasons, not even a week, a day,
A single moment when bud-burst is at its height;

And the white *Wisteria, floribunda Alba,*
Which grows in Monet's garden in Giverny,
Spills over the sidewalk onto East King Street
As it does over that luminous Japanese bridge.

Robin holds a weightless sable pointed round,
Transferring bright daubs of color to paper,
As if the brush is murmuring sweet matins;
Light comes down to dance on its glowing tip.

We paint what we see and what we don't, she said,
The visible and the invisible. And after a time
A clarity begins to emerge, a heightened alertness:
The ecstatic brush-tip transfiguration.

The Freighter

I will not call it karma; but things have a way
Of coming home: an old habit thoughtlessly taken up,
Like that garter snake I once trapped with a forked stick
And clutched behind its flat little head,

That wrapped itself so tightly around my wrist
I did not know how to release it. And this new habit
That I have come to enjoy more and more,
Of wasting time, of spending a perfectly good day

Buried in mindless contemplation of clouds
And sea surfaces, and gannets swooping down
Lazily to touch the bright shimmering sparkle,
And why their alabaster wings are tipped ink-black;

And why this afternoon I am filled with such joy
And such dread: the gulls can be laughing, or sneering.
For surely there must be some recompense for idleness,
Some tightening grip, some sure reckoning.

All day I have been watching through my binoculars
A freighter coming into the Morehead Channel;
It crawls unhurriedly between the channel markers
Swerving not an inch in its willful course.

On the blue horizon it is brighter than rust,
Blood-orange, mandarin red. I struggle in vain
To read the approaching name on its distant hull,
Still one step beyond the margin of sight.

Picking Blackberries on Yellow Mountain Road

It is Sunday morning and we should be in church
Instead of here on this unpaved road, cups in hand,
Picking blackberries on Yellow Mountain Road;
The succulent hours hanging silent before us.

We park the car under tall shade, and wander so far
That we have to backtrack what seems like miles,
Going from patch to patch in dappled light;
The dark alcoves where the gnats drone high and thin

And the sun-drenched openings, where the berries
Are sweet and tiny hard, only four or five nubs;
Absorbed and silent we work in peace, returning only
To pour our offerings into the common bowl.

Fingers sticky and stained wine-red, we wander along;
When suddenly we come to the mother patch,
Surprised in a shady place we nearly overlooked,
Big berries dangling dark beneath the spreading branches,

So tender and ripe for our touch that they tumble
Into cupped hands at the gentlest bump, like prayers
Unexpectedly answered, blessings untrammeled by
     suffering,
Hands filled to overflowing with humble blackberries.

70

Cherohala Skyway

Morning mist lingers in the valleys,
The nameless peaks of Snowbird turn pink
As I run at dawn along the Skyway,

Remembering why I chose to live here,
To run this particular path, high above the jewel lakes
Where eye is lifted and spirit soars.

Two doves see me coming and hop to a rocky spur;
Silence lies like the cool of the mountain,
Like dew in the grass, and only my footsteps,

My heart beating, give tempo to the rising day.
It is easy here to want to rededicate a life
To the solace of the piano, the sacrament of pencil

And paper, the gentle touch of love.
A certain elevation has been reached, and here
The road descends in a gentle, unending grade.

The Principles of Photography

1.

First do no harm, O Doctor
Of Photography. The world as you see it
Cannot be improved. Sunlight
Slants through the hazy morning in thick curtains
With as much glory as there can ever be.

2.

The rules on the surface are not complicated.
Diameter of lens, aperture, exposure –
All irrelevant. Technology begins
With the nub of a pencil, and ends
With a digital image on the internet.

3.

Beware of double and triple exposure,
Deliberate unfocus, rose-colored filter
Of eye and camera and mind: trick poetry.
Show us instead what you see in that
Single perfect moment of immortality.

4.

The red barn is one example:
It is what it is, standing in the tenuous haze
Of an August morning, falling roof undulating
In counterpoint to the basso continuo of mountains.
I was responsible for no more than opening the shutter.

72

5.

Why do I love these falling buildings?
The great kudzu plantations of South Carolina,
Green triumphant, skulls and bones gleaming in the brush,
The siren song of gravity.
One day I too will collapse.

6.

Look as closely as you can:
Distance is an illusion. Motes of dust
Drift in thick curtains across vast rooms;
The moon and the planets balance on the tips
Of tiny mountains.

Santeetlah Lake

We slid our canoes onto Santeetlah that morning,
As miraculously buoyant as the water striders,
Deep water green as a tabby's eye.

There was plenty of time, we had nowhere to be,
And the hours rippled out expansively around us,
Turning into blind coves, ending in little creeks.

The water so still: nothing but the gentle wake
Fanning out behind us, and the concentric circles
As bass broke the surface for dragonflies.

We glided over the skeletons of fallen trees,
Rock cairns flickering in the antediluvial green,
Ghostly stumps remembered in a dream.

Yes, this morning there was plenty of time,
Your hair burning copper, your bright vest,
The sweet kiss of your oar as it struck the water,

And the forgotten shore sliding alongside
Where the men and women we used to know so well
Took journeys from one place to another.

On One's Daughter Reading Milosz

I dreamt that I was descending a mountain pass
High above the Issa Valley, in Lithuania;
Long-stemmed purple flowers nodded along the way,
Musky fragrances strange to me yet close,
As if I had known them all my life.

You were walking with me, brother I never met,
You who saw so much more of this century than I,
Yet could focus my attention on a single sensation,
A blacksmith shop where hot iron sizzled cold,
Your feet in the dirt. This glory.

Now my daughter is reading your poems;
Her toes are scrunched up in that same dirt,
She smells the horses and the golden dung
In a country that no longer exists. What joy,
To hear her pronounce your name, Milosz.

Church bells toll softly in the valley below,
Fog hangs above the river in morning light.
In my dream, I hand to her the only gift I have:
Dog-eared poems in an obscure book,
Words of truth and love and freedom.

The Ages of Man

It turned out I was wrong, after all. I had learned
The seven ages of man from Jacques, *All the world's*
A stage, he said; but today it was all about
Retirement design solutions and preset upsides,

From a pair of fast-talking, likeable young brothers
Selling hybrid annuities in a roomful of retirees
Who were trying to improve their confidence in these
Volatile market conditions (or, like me, enjoy a free
    dinner).

Low-light ambiance, the quiet bustle of young women
In name-tagged vests in the whispering background,
Preparing to direct us to the buffet in the next room.
Not yet in *my lean and slippered pantaloon,* still

I wondered if these women listened at the door
As we were power-pointed through three ages of man –
Accumulation, preservation and consumption,
    distribution –
And imagined how they might play a part on that distant
    stage.

I wandered down the hall during intermission,
And watched the evening exacting its sure commission
On the waning day, the courtyard garden June-green,
Manicured by a team of polite Hispanic gardeners.

But this green day will crash into winter, even here
At this four-star resort; this garden will fall into the sere,
In quiet dialogue with oblivion. And I, too, will play my
    part,
Straining to hear the prompter's urgent whisper.

Fourth of July

Our old dog cowered shell-shocked,
Nose under the bed, while the bright artillery
Shouted destruction from a high placement
Right in the heart of our summer town.

She knew it was unnatural, this barrage of horror
Exploding into flowers in the cool night-sky.
What could it mean but bullets, and bigger bullets?
What could it mean but pain and death?

Yet citizens had set up chairs on the funeral home lawn;
Veterans wore peaked hats; children swirled sparklers.
We watched this display from a distance, you and I.
I always thought about my brother (Da Nang, 1966).

How he told me about his friend who talked to the dead;
Loading body bags onto choppers, he would
Shake hands and introduce himself, ask them where they
Hailed from: the little courtesies of the insane.

I knew the real cost of these dirty fireworks,
As they wasted upward with a hollow *whoosh.*
The chrysanthemum and peonies, spiders and horsetails;
Pretty palms and diadems breaking apart forever.

When it was over, our dog crept out, whimpering
    uneasily.
We stood on the porch and watched the white smoke
Drift away over the trees. Fireflies fell to the wet lawn
Like wounded stars, an infirmary of clover and plantain.

This must be patriotism, then: watching from a chair
The distant displays of light. Down the road a neighbor

Was putting on his own tawdry little show: bottle
   rockets,
And a few sad cherry bombs from a roadside stand.

Savannah

[For Connie Houston]

Wide and deep the sea and the sky,
And so soothing, the gentle rocking of the boat.
The long days, the long nights,
The phosphorescence gleaming deep below,
And the sea birds drifting far overhead.

I have heard that sailors used to tumble
Out of their boats and into the sea,
For no reason at all, simply
Overcome by the vastness,
Like children rolling over in their cribs.

And this same tumbling over
Afflicts space travelers:
A Soyuz astronaut was inside,
While his brother
Floated at the end of his tether;

Then he stole a look at the infinite,
He peeked outside the little ship, and
Began to drift
Silently away,
Until his brother caught his foot.

Drift away now, Connie,
Into the distances of sea and sky;
You can let yourself go home
On this quiet street in Savannah,
The whisper of Spanish moss in the light breeze.

Lake Tohopekaliga

1. *Sunlight*

Running along the shore of Lake Tohopekaliga,
Even at this early hour, is a struggle.

The sun is a tyrant whose presence is felt
Even when it is gone. An hour before dawn,

Night evaporates; the shadows crawl away
Up into mossy oaks and jangling palms;

The cool waters sink in murk and mud.
And this Dominance rises already hot.

2. *Water*

To move is to sweat in this daunting place;
In moments I am drenched: water in the air,

In the lake, in the marshes and swales,
In the reeds where the wading birds poise.

I realize that Lake Tohopekaliga
Has soaked into everything around it,

And this shoreline is but a temporary,
Conditional accommodation with water.

3. *Wading Birds*

The wading birds at Lake Tohopekaliga
Ibis and egret, brown and slender white,

Stand as still and spiky as reeds, bobbing
Like whirligigs made of sticks and wire,

Without volition. They watch me run by –
Heavy of breath, pounding out a difficult,

Obscure course – with cold black eye,
Their thoughts a ripple in bright water.

Drought in July

These long rainless days, one after another:
The grass turns yellow and crinkles underfoot,
And all the little streams have long since dried up.

One can see and measure the scant surface water,
But water cradled underground is a blessing
We tap guiltily, with parsimonious pump and pipe –

It is like a fault forgiven too often,
A favor we cannot return. Only the thunderclouds
That rise up with such promise each afternoon

Can redeem this thirst, but they so often amount
To nothing: leaves blown white, outsized drops
Pockmarking the dust. Rumbling to north, or to south.

And still the withered stalk and stem,
The shriveled leave, the ground as hard as justice,
Do not give up hope. Even after long days,

After nights deathly still; in despair of twig,
In hopelessness of blackened leaves, these
Dry branches nurture a little sap, a quiver,

A core of surprise. It is like soft laughter
On the porch of the funeral home, where
Friends have come out to watch the heat lightning,

To listen to the katydids, to feel the evening air
Grow cool and heavy as it gathers itself up,
Waiting for rain to explode on the roof.

Summer Nights

Summer nights, the familiar foliage
Closes round. The air is cool and musky,
And I dream of ripe pears and pipe organs.

I sleep lightly, awakened by languid rain,
Or the bugle of an errant hound. I lie still,
And listen, savoring the night.

It is late July, and suddenly I become aware
That the katydids have begun to speak:
They creak forward from the fabric of night,

Out of the soughing limbs of the hemlocks,
The swish and rustle of laurel, ratcheting
Mechanical, as if tightening, and tightening,

And tightening again. So this slovenly summer.
This paunch of weeds, this overripeness,
Is winding up, and winding down. See:

A sliver of moon appears in the trees,
And swivels its dish to hear this creaking
Of solstice wheeling past.

Building Walls

They were cold culls from Elberton,
Ransomed from the scrap heap,
Not good enough for headstones but
Sufficient for this crooked little wall.

I used to think I was good at stonework;
Choosing with care the exactest stone,
Like the perfect word in the perfect quatrain
Stand firm, good wall, I wrote long ago,

*In this sunlight into which I have called you
And the shadows of poplars not yet sprouted;
Dig in your heels and lean into the earth,
Thick with moss and thrift.* So I stacked them,

Two stones on one, one stone on two, in the
Time-honored way, with plenty of weep-holes;
I mixed mortar by hand with a rusty hoe
In my battered wheelbarrow crusted with use.

Here was syntax I could trust, unlike words,
That skitter and slip like living things,
Like the dappled sunlight under these trees
That shift and change when the wind blows.

Hard work and little to show for it. Still,
I cobbled these stubborn stones together
To hold back the weighty soil, or to enclose
Some small holy space I wanted to make.

A Long Summer

At last this long summer is nearing an end:
The obscure dawn breaking free from the night,
The morning fog growing heavy with the milky light.
The midday lassitude. The garden is unruly,
Its mildewed vines slithering into the wet grass,
And the spotted fruit ripening too quickly on the trees;
Even the mountaintops are nearsighted and dim.

Yellowjackets have constructed a nest in the walls;
They drone a barely audible hum, low and ominous,
And now and then they work their way inside.
Every evening, thunderstorms convene in the west;
The air booms, and steaming rain rattles the downspouts.
Umbrellas never dry, swollen doors warp and stick;
The blade is dull and the heaped hay wastes in the fields.

It is August, and the days and nights are past ripening,
The Rose of Sharon has bloomed in profusion:
Too much summer, too much goodness. The green
     pastures
Are lying down in righteousness, and the cows on the
     hillside
Are all facing in one direction, listening, listening:
It is the end of indolence, the beginning of the Requiem.
The katydids hear it too: they are marking time.

And suddenly one morning it is cool, and dry, and sharp,
And a new moon lingers in the west, thin and icy.
Morning is like a lover who has eaten an apple,
The first apple of the season. Her breath is sweet,
And I can taste it in her mouth when I kiss her.
Her hair is long and red and it spills onto the pillow.
I take her in my arms and embrace her once again.

Learning to Pay Attention

I don't know why it is said we *pay* attention,
As if we carry a burden of debt, both principle
And interest. This August morning I climbed
The familiar switchback path up the mountain,

Paying the day its due all along the way.
The sighing branches, the overhead leaf-rustle,
Chirp of bird, underfoot crunch of twig and pebble.
Jewelweed – spotted touch-me-not –

And Joe Pye weed bowing on tall stalks
Foretold an early fall. I reached the summit
And saw that clouds had settled overnight
Recumbent in the valley in a soft luminous swoon,

Spreading out abundantly between the peaks.
It seemed as if there was all the time in the world
This morning, an inheritance of endless daylight.
The fog began to roll slowly up the slopes

Of Satulah Mountain, and out in the open valley
Soft tendrils climbed into the sky overhead;
They were prayers of hope, this wealth of daylight,
This providence of fragrant summer air.

Down East Flood

It rained as never before in this city by the ocean,
Out where there is no high ground at all; none.
An outstretched hand remembers, waist high.

The water is bulging, slopping against
The pilings under the boardwalk, dark and green,
In uneasy acquaintance with what lies beneath.

And along the causeway, Bogue Sound so close
To the road, a little wave could brim ahead of us,
Settling there in treacherous reflection of sky.

They all have stories to tell about that day,
The kind they will pass on to children,
To grandchildren: heirlooms of calamity.

Imagine water coming in the first floor, he said,
Climbing, stealthy as a burglar, up the stairs,
As you flee out the bedroom window onto the roof;

The bookcase in the library the first to drown,
The Tempest, and *Ulysses*, family Bible, paperbacks,
Floating gently to the surface before sinking

Out of memory. Is this the way civilization
Ends? Soggy books, desperate flight; little boats
Rocking in the dark flood, the final tide.

Pickles

Watermelon rinds, thick and sweet as summer,
And okra, peppers, pale artichoke hearts, even
Pumpkin slices: You can pickle anything, he said,
Handing me a clinking paper sack of mason jars,

The fruits of his solitary craft. And I handed him
My own homebrewed beer, a recent ESB
And a fine Belgian Tripel (my own little sideline),
We eyed each other a little warily, I thought,

Until we had tasted each other's work, and approved.
He had worked in the Pentagon, and I wondered
About this soldier and his pickles, jarred and sealed,
Long lost seasons preserved at their peak,

Brought to some small conclusion. I had my own reasons
For brewing strong beer. These modest affirmations of
    free men,
Colleagues and friends; he drank my beer in appreciation,
I lined up his jars on my bookshelf, where golden light
    gleamed

Through the limpid sweet-sour juice, these perfect
    specimens
Suspended in glory, redeemed from decay. I put them
    with
My books of poetry, bookends for Bishop, Stevens,
    Milosz,
Where they glowed with the quiet miracle of
    transformation.

Read Me From the Book of Glory

[A song in memory of Leonard Cohen – 1934-2016]

Read me from the Book of Glory,
Pages burning bright;
Let me hear your soft voice whisper
Read me through the night.

Read to me, those sweet old verses
Dog-eared in the book;
The home of my remembering
The journey that I took.

> *Turn the pages slowly,*
> *Turn them day by day;*
> *Turn the pages slowly,*
> *Read my life away.*

Remind me of the narrow passages,
The places where I went;
All the twists and turns I took,
Meandering intent.

Read me undiscovered worlds,
The pages toward the end;
Fresh as winter sky swept clean
Of all impediment.

> *Turn the pages slowly,*
> *Turn them day by day;*
> *Turn the pages slowly,*
> *Read my life away.*

Show me bright and vivid figures
I barely understand;
The dangling scarf of daylight
On a twisted branch of sand.

Fling wide the nets of silver and gold,
Speak of the Fishermen Three;
Let me gaze with wonder again
At the moon on the lustrous sea.

Turn the pages slowly,
Turn them day by day;
Turn the pages slowly,
Read my life away.

Yes, let me into your book again,
The secret pages of hiding;
Comfort me with liquid song
In the place of your abiding.

Read me from the Book of Glory,
Whisper in my ear;
Keep at bay the terrible silence
Hold me close and near.

Turn the pages slowly,
Turn them day by day;
Turn the pages slowly,
Read my life away.

90

Read Me From the Book of Glory

Richard Betz

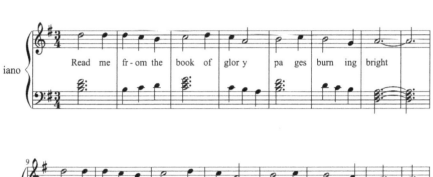

Read me fr - om the book of glor y pa ges burn ing bright

Let me he - ar your soft voice whis-per read me through the night

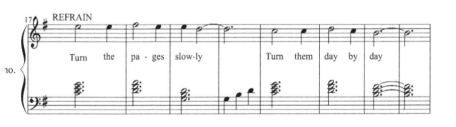

REFRAIN

Turn the pa - ges slow-ly Turn them day by day

Turn the pa - ges slow-ly Read my life A - way

Witness

The rain is cold. A conspiracy of weeds
Has brought low the garden strings and stakes.
Crooked tomatoes dangle from a blackened stem,
And holes have been bored in the bloated squash.

It is late September, time to give up on gardens,
To relinquish what has not come round;
Now worm and rot have settled in
In this brief season between frost and frost.

Round an untended tree lies a waste of apples,
Mazed and mottled in the copper leaves,
Fruit that was never picked nor tasted,
Bruised before it fell. I know it well,

These little cadavers, this ancient tree.
In the cold rain I walk and I watch,
I slide and smush in the sweet musk of decay,
The only witness in this inaccessible remove.

Sleight of Moon

I'm in cahoots tonight with that sly old moon,
Winking through the branches of the dogwood tree:

That scuppernong moon chiming through the night,
Saffron moon, strolling in the starry arcade,

Mum moon tacking through the sailcloth clouds,
Hovering over the matter-of-fact darkness.

She casts blue shadows through the uplifting trees.
But what if she had no more tricks up her sleeve,

No prestidigitation of sound or sense,
Here where I wander in fields already gleaned,

Where the great uneasiness spreads underfoot
Like cold water seeping through earthbound shoes.

Sermons in Stone

"Sweet are the uses of adversity."
– *As You Like It*, Act II, Scene I

It may well be that memory responds to stress.
So I wrestle with another piece of Shakespeare,
Taking the long road into Arden Forest.
Are not these woods more free from what?

Always a word or two cludes me,
A line remains unrecited, a stitch is dropped,
"It might have been. It should have been."
The churlish chiding of conscience,

The horse that walks away and will not return.
Bitter is the peril of forgetfulness,
The sudden insight fading as quickly as snow melting
On the surface of running waters. So commit,

Commit this October day to memory:
The sweet circle of leaves around the feet of the maple
Like a coppery negligee fallen to the ground,
The sudden turns of light and passion flashing,

The grand applause of the late afternoon,
And in the lengthening shadows of the day
Diagonally across the road an exaltation of leaves
Released, at last – free! – exonerated by the wind.

Commit these consolations of molten light,
Hard-won in the adversity of the struggle:
The familiar sickle of the new moon cutting low
The icy sound it makes in the unfamiliar day.

Gardener's Confession

Forgive me Father for I have doubted;
I no longer believe in the bodily resurrection.

It is late November and all the leaves have fallen
And I know that they will not rise again.

I prepare them now for humble composting,
The glistening earthworms working in deep silence.

I understand the dark secrets of decomposition;
I have learned how to make good rich soil,

And when to plant seeds in a new garden,
In another country beyond this cathedral of doubt.

Forgive me, for I once believed this glory would last
Forever: how those leaves did shimmer with ecstasy;

They burned and thirsted for light, thrust high
On branches held to heaven like platters of butterflies.

And it was enough for the day, without those visions
Of everlasting fruit dangling at the end of time.

Let the heartbreaking musk of rotting leaves keep me
        honest:
It is enough to work in humility and peace.

Sowing Winter Rye

The sky was a broken promise,
The long field – stubbled with Golgotha stumps
And stray weeds nodding on their stalks –
Was desolate in mid-October.

We read the history which the used ground holds
As we advanced: there was the crushed paper cup
That softened the hot September sun;
The green lizard under a yellow leaf;

And that is where, when I stopped to mop my brow,
It first occurred to me that this might come
To nothing: that the empty field, corrupted into gullies,
Might wear on untended under a thin winter moon.

But this day there was work to be done. The field
Widened before us as we walked. The battered pail
Swung heavily with blond rye: and my hand,
Plunging in, seemed to say yes, yes,

And we broadcast this message as we walked,
The faint growl of a tractor, the rustle of birds behind,
Binding the broken October sky together again,
Swinging big golden arcs before us in the air.

Farewell to Arrowood Road

Farewell, old house: stand firm
On your precarious cairns, and shelter others

From summer rain and winter frost.
I have followed the shadow of the hill,

The path of the moon, and the wheel of stars
From your dilapidated porch. The north star:

There, just between those trees. Stand against
The wind that has blown all day, that has

Stirred up the October leaves in a rush,
And called us up the road with an insistent power.

We'll leave a kettle of water ready on the stove,
And sweep the walk as we go.

October Light

How little I know of the world, after all.
I think that I will never understand

The simple rustling of the October leaves,
Wind chimes of dry husks and paper lanterns;

Or truly know color that quickens the eye,
Shimmering against the cloudless skies:

The leaves are to light
What church bells are to sound;

The reluctance as they cling,
One by one, to bare branches,

So hard to let go of this blessed realm
Of light and motion and music.

Or the wind that stirs them up,
Whirling and dancing to inscrutable music,

Dispersing them in the cold air
Like an instrument of revelation.

The way the moon climbs hand over hand
Through the emptying branches,

Breaking free at last. I gaze dumbly
At the great toys of astrophysics, and ask:

Is it not enough to simply savor
This magnificence of October,

These images gleaming under water
Like brilliant pebbles in a stream bed?

Or am I compelled to examine closely,
To seize the brighter hints, the most

Perfect specimens, and stuff them in my pocket?
See. Already they have begun to fade.

Autumn Piece

A fresh wind is blowing,
Cool as Oriental porcelain,

Stirring up the first leaves of autumn,
Scattering chaff of weed, detritus

Of another obesity of season. There
Is a thin, an elegant edge

To the air tonight. It is a cup
Of sharp, clear tea, that

Nudges the mind into business.
A new generation of owls plies the wood:

Their cries come to the ear mingled with
The usual jangle of woodsmoke, star, and hymn.

Wide Awake

After all this time
I expected to know more
Than these few lean precepts,
Prized from ordinary days;

I expected to say more
Than merely grace:
Grace for the burning trees,
The shining rain.

This day in October
Reminded me what Broad Daylight means:
Pinching up every crumb of day
With the tines of a rusty fork,

Greedy for the endless solace
Of earthly sustenance,
The taste of the purely physical
On the tip of my tongue.

The empirical sun
Blazed away anything that
Came between us, any impediment
To complete wakefulness.

And even the lopsided moon
Was still awake overhead,
Rising higher and higher and higher
In glorious insomnia.

The Wrong Things

All my life I have loved the wrong things:
The crooked crows feet in the corner of the eyes,
The freckled apple that fell overnight,
The opulent brown bruise on its underside
So soft and rotten beneath my finger.

I loved the snow when it was almost gone,
The profaned ice on the unraked leaves,
The heel of my boot slipping in the mud;
I loved the blindness at the bottom of the garden
And the memory of the dead tangled vines.

April is beautiful when it's all wrong,
The daffodils toppled over in the late snow,
And the bent and the lost branches
Upturned poking in the mayhem of the yard.
The doomed. The broken and defeated.

I loved that cold rain that fell all day long
And did not relent, and never relented.
And the upside-down moon soaking wet,
Sprawled like cancer in its unkindness,
Rotting in the stubbled cornfield rows.

The wrong turns that led me into darkness,
The wrong words that I yearned to hear again,
And the secrets places where I loved to go alone:
Crows rattled across the empty sky at dusk,
Winging their way south to north.

But what can I do, after all. The heart is
Intractable; it has a will of its own,
And the naked eye, with its insistent power,
Peering intently into the dark corners, unblinking
In the penetrating blindness of its love.

November

Just when I think all the colors have been exhausted
Another outrageous sunset sprawls across the sky;
Charleston pink on baby blue – a child's bassinet –

Or another corona of gold glowing behind Rabun Bald,
But posed now as a question, in a different context than
     before;
And there burned-out trees black against the roaring fire.

Some evenings it seems as if anything is possible,
As if the last remaining leaves could burst into darkness,
Or the sound of bagpipes could be a bright, crisp color

And not a mournful sound; this wide discourse
Could have no bounds, but go on forever,
Beyond these scattered clouds, palette-daubed.

O glory of day, dark solace of night:
There is nothing that cannot be imagined,
Nothing. Now I stand on the very edge,

Looking out on both sides of the same evening.
Now it is possible to imagine a new November
Out of these impossible shards of color and sound.

December

That rainy December seemed filled with powerful images;
Whether portents of the future or memories of the past,
I could not say. The last bright festival pennants were

Taken down overnight in a cold rain. Sodden scarecrows
Bowed from their stakes of bamboo, and black crows
Rose suddenly from roadside carrion like dark smoke;

But along the bleak horizon, light sloshed over the edge
Unexpectedly, in a long crooked gleam of promise:
Simple shelter and a warm fire, laughter's gentle cascade.

This America was losing its way on the nightly news,
Devouring itself with greed, forgetting its heritage.
Shiny spheres of gold and silver dangled from dead
      boughs,

And costumed carolers gathered in public places to sing,
Stirring old memories and awaking new dreams.
Strong ale was brewing in the closet. I wanted to

Give up foolish things, and hold fast to what mattered.
Why did I want more? More than peace and grace,
More than I deserved? When there was less and less.

The Blessing of the Snow Shovels

Bless, O Lord, our most earnest snow shovels
This cold bright morning, when the wind is biting
And the diamonds are scattered on the deep;

The church is riding like a tall ship
On a sea of sight, and we have arrived together,
Six or seven of us, wielding scoops and blades,

To uncover the buried paths, to clear the way
Through the knee-high drifts, each of us beginning
At a different place, and working his way in solitude

In the dazzle of morning, in the bright, bright
Blindness of day, wrapped up against the cold,
Working forward stroke by stroke.

But what is that deep, eerie sound?
The grinding of machinery frozen in the night,
The rasping and screeching of iron on iron,

Like old doors that have rusted shut,
Or a voice that has long been silent,
Suddenly opening into stuttering sound:

It is the music of the steeple chimes,
Awakening with a moan, rising and breaking
Into familiar doxologies. They buoy us up

In our simple labor. Bless, O Lord,
This rhythm of back and legs and arms, this joy,
This patient work our only theology.

Clear Ice

A car went off a narrow bridge, crooked as a crack,
So many years ago nobody can remember when,
And plunged to the very bottom of the deep creek
That fed this watery vault we called Turtle Pond.

The unrecovered body fed boyhood imagination:
We thought we spied a skeleton in a flannel shirt
Far below a surface where water striders skated,
Down in the mud, daylight tarnished cold bronze.

We wanted to get to the bottom of things,
To know how deep, how far, how long ago it was.
When winter came, I remember walking out on ice
Perfectly clear: the bottom unnervingly revealed.

We whispered our way out inch by inch,
Tiptoeing in a ballet of icy acrophobia, listening
For the crack that would plunge us downward,
Flailing arms scrabbling at impossible surfaces;

Suspended between two terrifying worlds:
Dark sky above, limpid depths below;
So close to drowning, daring each other to go farther
And farther, out on this delicate sustaining miracle.

Five Egrets Descending in Snow

[From the Japanese woodblock print by Ohara Koson]

There is a reason they call it the
Dead of winter, when everything
Stops, when some things end.

Ten days below freezing:
The forgotten rain gauge shattered
From the bottomless cold.

The rhododendron leaves curled up,
Tight mittened fists, revealing mere
Millimeters to the sharp air.

Snow shrouded the branches,
The skeletal branches that bowed down
Under the weightless snow.

Into this condition, in the evening,
A congregation of egrets descended,
One after another, floating gently down,

Dark blue falling into light blue,
Their thin legs dangling like twigs,
Their unblinking eyes staring ahead,

A visitation as silent as the falling snow.
One. Two. Three. Four. Five.
Descending in snow.

The lowest one has his wings raised high,
Preparing to finally come to rest
On the dead ground invisible below.

The Ice Storm

The ice storm materialized matter-of-factly in the night
Without fanfare; soft metallic tapping on the roof
Different in kind from rain, as cancer is different
From passing sickness. The slow, clinging weight,
Bent the little branches, sheathed round tightly like wire;
Ice softly slickened the deck in the gray morning light.

It reminded me of Elizabeth and Mel, and Sandra,
Weighed down separately, struggling through stages;
And Christine, holding her breath these days;
Pallid James with sunken cheeks, deflating with a sigh.
I carry their names with me throughout the day,
Running down the list. You could call it a prayer.

I went outside to consider this bleak new world,
The ghostly sheen on the rhododendron leaves,
And the pine-tops every few minutes cracking,
Torn limbs letting go under the hopeless weight.
In a different season the sun might have broken through,
Water begun to trickle into stream and river and ocean;

But this ice has metastasized; it is here to stay,
Wreaking slow destruction by incremental weight,
Like points made in an argument – slowly, patiently –
That you realize you are losing, no matter how much
You once believed. Brokenness littered the yard,
And one by one I softly whispered their names.

A Hard Winter

We had forgotten what a hard winter was like,
The snow settling on the ground the long weeks,
The rhododendron leaves rolled up tight-fisted;
Even the camels in the Christmas parade seemed
Ill at ease, and Harris Lake, frozen for the first time
In fifteen years and thronged with ice-skaters,
Seemed to resent the bonfire on the southern shore.

A sullen north wind kept blowing and blowing
With an immense rawness redolent of jet stream,
Windswept arctic tundra, and revolving globe,
Cutting through fleece as if it were nothing.
We had forgotten how painful fingers could become,
Bare skin numb, fumbling at keys and latches.
Even speech was slurred by the numbing cold.

An elderly man wandered away from his home and
Died of exposure. Nationwide, the Weather Channel
Totted up the taken lives credited to simple cold,
As if it were an ominous entity merciless in intent.
Outside in the snow where the summer hammock hung
A red cardinal scratched among the husks of perennials,
Its tiny footprints pointing this way, and that way.

We wished that we had more southern exposure,
Big stones close to the house, warm to the touch,
And terraces drinking up sunlight behind double glass.
The cat would curl up in a window seat and sleep all day,
Purring green dreams, while hot chocolate steam
Would curl lazily from two fat porcelain mugs.
We would become the children we once longed to be.

Christmas Poems

1. *Carol*

All the lights are on tonight,
All the candles lit;
The star is in the window where
The little village sits.

These decorations, so familiar,
Year to year:
The words of love and kindness
We need to hear.

Christmas carols sung outside
In the frosty night,
Gathered round the welcome door,
Warm and golden bright.

2. *Emptiness*

Now the thicket of summer is spent
And emptiness finds its way in,
Opening vistas of wine-red sunsets,
Blue moons, and winter stars.

Father Abraham: did you gaze, too,
At the limitless stars? Did you
Look beyond the bleating and the dung
To distances and dreams no longer

Concealed? Across the wide plains,
The lights of heaven are revealed.
A wind stirs up, cold as the moon,
And moves through the branches silently.

3. *Shadows*

Doubt creeps in, the nagging dog,
Shadow passing over on the sunniest of days,

Hesitation when the time is ripe,
Sadness in the smile, stone in the shoe,

Whisper in the cupped hand. Free us,
O mighty words of truth: help us see
The light beneath the shadow, the
Immutable. Help us to persevere

Through pain and suffering. There is
No limit to what can be endured:

Strength is as available as the sweet,
Sweet air we breath.

4. *Sweets*

In the bitterness of winter we console ourselves
With sweet oranges and nuts, citron to nibble,
Cookies shaped like reindeer and fir trees.

Last night the wind howled, the stars were
Displaced, and branches strewn across the road,
But our gingerbread house stood unshaken

On its lawn of coconut. Candied fruit
Allays the bleakness, and the jar in Tennessee
Is filled with sugared pecans.

5. *Pfeffernusse*

There must be at least one Christmas cookie
That is German, difficult to pronounce,
Hard as an innkeeper's heart,
Filled with spices strange and pungent,

Pepper and clove and crystallized orange,
Carried on camelback in tinkling caravans,
Strong brandy by the campfire at night,
Rolled in the fine sugar of mercy.

6. *Snowmelt*

I like the snow just as much when it's half-gone,
Dimpled and stained with mud, showing the teeth marks
Of tire treads and the lumps of fender ice;

I like when it melts into the blackened mud,
And turns the northern slopes into speckled ponies.
Footprints of small animals are quarter notes

Escaping bar and staff, and the even,
Precise accretion has fallen into crooked caps,
Or big floppy hats long out of fashion;

I like it then, between the last snow and
The next, the idealist and the cynic,
The hopelessness and the promise.

7. *Sonnet*

Christmas Eve candlelight service sonnet:
We sing familiar hymns to babe and star,
Light in the darkness, and take the sacrament
By intinction - two by two, body and blood.

Then we turn out the lights and from the
Advent candle we light our own, one by one
Little white tapers in the big old church,
Each candle thrust through a paper saucer.

As the flame wavers in the darkness,
I notice there is a little shadow, always,
A shadow, wobbling around the very core
Of my candle, cast by the candle itself:

Darkness at the very heart of light.
We sing Silent Night, Silent Night.

8. *Incurving*

Now is the time
For candles in the dark;
For listening to parables
Of hoarfrost, and sunrise

Flooding colorless December
With life and light.
Archangels in the trees above,
A sliver of moon

High and sharp and incontestable,
Preparing the way: see how it
Incurves upon itself icily
In a new and wonderful way.

Acknowledgements

First and foremost, I would like to thank my loving wife Martha for reading early drafts, providing valuable advice, and encouraging me to publish this my first book of poetry. I would also like to thank a sharp-eyed nonagenarian aunt, Anne Sellers, for proof-reading the final manuscript. Another generous aunt, Lizette Pryor, made it possible for us to spend an annual sabbatical at her beach place, where much of my inspiration and writing took place. The North Carolina Literary Review has encouraged me over the years as well, and published the following poems which were finalists or honorably mentioned in the James Applewhite Poetry Prize:

Perfect Pitch
Splitting Oak
Maundy Thursday
Branch Drop
The Sweetness of Doing Nothing
Picking Blackberries on Yellow Mountain Road
Wide Awake
Clear Ice

Finally, I would like to say a special thanks to my friend Dr. Randolph P. Shaffner, who reviewed and kindly wrote a Foreword for this book, and to Thomas Rain Crowe, who also reviewed it and has encouraged me. Their insights and their suggestions were invaluable.

.

CPSIA information can be obtained
at www.ICGtesting.com
Printed in the USA
BVHW060102160721
611886BV00003B/59